THE LAST WHITE HOUSE AT THE END OF THE ROW OF WHITE HOUSES

THE LAST WHITE HOUSE AT THE END OF THE ROW OF WHITE HOUSES

MICHAEL E. CASTEELS

Invisible Publishing
Halifax & Picton

Library and Archives Canada Cataloguing in Publication

Casteels, Michael e., 1985-, author
    The last white house at the end of the row of white houses / Michael e. Casteels.

Poems.
Issued in print and electronic formats.
ISBN 978-1-926743-81-3 (paperback).--ISBN 978-1-926743-82-0 (html)

    I. Title.

PS8605.A8745L37 2016   C811'.6   C2016-905494-2
                                               C2016-905495-0

Edited by Leigh Nash

Cover and interior design by Megan Fildes | Typeset in Laurentian
With thanks to type designer Rod McDonald

Printed and bound in Canada

Invisible Publishing | Halifax & Picton
www.invisiblepublishing.com

We acknowledge the support of the Canada Council for the Arts which last year invested $20.1 million in writing and publishing throughout Canada.

Canada Council   Conseil des Arts
for the Arts   du Canada

|

The moths settle on the windowpane:
small pale telegrams from the world.

— Tomas Tranströmer

HOUSE OF STICKS

I open the door and I am greeted by a wolf.

The wolf opens its jaws, shows off my half-eaten grandmother.

Grandmother opens her hands, reveals a blue egg.

The egg hatches. I step out and can hardly believe my eyes.

THE SAME OLD STORY

Once Upon a Time involves a horse. It involves
a heralding trumpet, a voice catapulting over palisades.
Once Upon a Time involves the last Tasmanian tiger
seeking refuge in a laundromat. It involves a punching bag
thrashing in its sleep. Once Upon a Time involves
purple loosestrife swashbuckling in the swale. It involves
the estuary ablitz with fledglings. Once Upon a Time
involves a pigeon and genie. It involves a goldfinch
made of gold, a world made of crumbs, a broom swooping
into the cellar. Once Upon a Time involves wild dogs
carousing among wildflowers. It involves the detective's
hunch, the poltergeist in the cathedral. Once Upon a Time
involves a fox curled in its den by the meadow. It involves
a fox curled inside this fox's womb. Once Upon a Time involves
an umbrella adrift at sea. It involves a bowling ball hurtling
through outer space, a Zamboni constellating into the zodiac.

FOR THE PRICE OF A QUARTER

On this side of the river the horses walk freely among us. You can see them trotting through city parks, or wandering downtown, drinking from fountains or staring into storefront windows. Last night I saw one at the movie theatre, watching a film. In one particularly harrowing scene a horse was pulling a wagonload of dead horses uphill in the rain. An evil-faced man barked orders and cracked a whip at the horse's flank. The horse kept slipping backwards, but dug its hooves in deeper and tried again. After the show I saw that same horse, the movie-going one, wandering the streets alone, its humungous head hung low. As it passed by the supermarket it stopped and gazed at a coin-operated kiddie-ride: a horse suspended in mid-gallop, paint flaking from its side, garbage cluttering its base. The horse sighed deeply and continued on, hooves clomping into the night. When the horse was out of sight, I approached the ride and slipped in a quarter. I climbed into the saddle and gripped the reins tightly. As music crackled from weathered speakers and the horse began surging forward I thought, "So this is what it feels like." It was more exhilarating than I'd imagined, but when the ride ended and I dismounted I suddenly felt filthy, like I'd committed a hideous crime. As I walked home everyone, both human and horse, eyed me suspiciously. Then, it began to rain.

THE RED LIGHT

I'm already late and speeding,
praying the light doesn't change.
It does and I stop.
I tap my fingers against the wheel,
twist dials on the dash. In the rear-view mirror
I examine the spaces between my teeth.
The light hasn't changed.
I rummage through the glovebox,
remembering the spearmint gum.
I count spare change in the ashtray.
Minutes pass. I consult the
owner's manual. I read it
cover to cover and still
the light remains. At sundown
I begin to worry. I take only
short sips from my water bottle.
I flick the high beams off and on,
signalling in Morse code. It's getting late.
Radio hosts abandon the airwaves.
I watch the moon drift overhead.

Night after night
the moon wanes
until crescent, and then
into nothing. I've been
counting the days on my
fingers and toes. Seasons
shift and skew. I engage the
wipers when it rains, crank the
defrost when it snows.
On humid summer evenings
I roll down the window
and let my arm dangle.
A faint breeze stirs my thoughts
and I wonder about Goldie.

Is she swimming in circles
or just floating in the archway
of that tiny plastic castle? I hope the water
is fresh, that her bowl is clean. I hope she wants
for nothing. And sitting here, bathed in the glow
of this godforsaken light, I wonder
if she'd even remember me.

PARTICLES

Subtract your elegy from my sonnet.
Extract the essence from the flora.
Impersonate the prime minister;
pretend you are a pig or some other
kind of swine. Gargle the wine to appear
knowledgeable. Reiterate your thesis. Ease
the speed of snowfall. Bellow from your
diaphragm. This diagram will illustrate how.
Did I tell you about my atoms? They are
like Lego. You can build a pirate ship or
a robot or a castle equipped with lasers or glow-
in-the-dark ghosts. Grammar is of
importance. The coffee was imported.
When you cough, cover your mouth.
Germs are nasty. Germans brew tasty beer.
Have you seen my beard? It's here, on my face.
There is no excuse for your lack of insight.
Did you see it? It was here on my face.

THE MAP

Somebody dropped a map on the sidewalk downtown and no one stopped to pick it up. Now it's dark, the streets are empty, and the map is alone. It shivers as the fingers of a heavy breeze grab the edge of a page and start pulling. The map spreads out in all directions. It crawls over fire hydrants and parked cars, mailboxes, phone booths. It climbs up lampposts and stop signs. It smothers buildings and bridges. The map unfolds until it blankets the entire city at a ratio of one-to-one.

The next morning, no one is late for work. Their keys are right where they left them. No one misplaces a wallet or searches for a missing sock. The lost dog arrives at the front door and barks to be let in. No one stops to ask for directions. No one honks a horn or slams on their brakes. Everything inhabits its own space and everything feels right at home. But the map, now one with its city, longs for a pocket to nestle in. It wants to be folded and pressed against another map, a map of some foreign city whose streets are beautifully unknown.

DINNER PARTY

After dinner the plates smash themselves against one another. The remains of the pork roast grunt and wriggle off the cutting board. The forks and knives slip into the cutlery drawer, feigning cleanliness. Wineglasses slosh and sway, one tips over, spewing its Pinot Noir. The white tablecloth rushes to the laundry room, flinging everything into the air with its exit. Wineglasses explode across hardwood, leftover casserole drips down the wall. A stray candle sets fire to the chairs. The table rears onto its hind legs and gallops out the front door. The hostess dabs the corner of her mouth with a lemon-scented serviette and smiles, as if everything were normal, which it is.

SONNET

The irises arrive, overgrowing the orchard,
the sultan seated beneath harvest.
Pupils bloom and dilate in this hinterland,
this salubrious work-in-progress. A pheasant
oscillates from treetop to treetop; the curtains
part and there she is, oh trembling heart,
oh hyperventilation! If I were a horse
I'd equilibrate, if a rhinoceros I'd radiate tungsten.
But I am only a salvaged typewriter
draped in seaweed; my bell no longer dings.
She is one dozen donuts. To blink would obliterate.
To drown in the ordnance of her synaesthesia I'd
punctuate this moment with a phalanx of ampersands.
I'd lasso that golden sphere you sometimes see in the sky.

ACT OF GOD

It was a dust storm, a tornado, dynamite. Windows shattered. Roofs blown right off. Saloon doors still swinging, playing cards drifting in the air. The train station stood on its side, the tracks twisted into knots. The corral posts splintered. The horses set running. Then came our marshal. "It was God robbed the bank," he said. "Well, what're you gonna do about it?" someone yelled, but the marshal was already flat disappeared, and that wasn't like him at all.

REMEMBER A BIRD

Remember a bird smacked into the living room window.
Among the geraniums it appeared tiny and broken,
but seconds later it ruffled its feathers and away it went.
When the dog is staring at you, listen. Listen also
to the lake, who speaks in stereo. You can go blind
from staring at the moon, though it may take all night.
Don't blink or you'll miss it, the exchanging days,
how seamless and lacustrine. On page 345 the dictionary
defines itself. Somewhere, there is a word for me,
for you, for the silhouette of a crane perched on a building
under construction. The dog is staring. Can you hear it?
It's like silence or that other thing, the sound
your shadow makes walking the dog's shadow.

THE ROBOT FACTORY

Parts of a robot lie on a conveyor belt. A robot welds on arms, another installs the head. A robot inserts a motherboard, solders wires. A robot screws light bulbs into sockets and sends the robot down the line. A robot leans toward another robot and mutters, "Is it five-thirty yet?" Management is aware of a growing discontent among the robots. A few robots sit in a boardroom and discuss solutions: longer breaks, soothing music, nature sounds. A robot sharpens a pencil. A robot prints confidential documents. Another robot shreds them. A robot sweeps the factory floor, collecting dust and bolts and small parts of robots. A robot rivets on legs, another inspects them for quality. A robot installs a motor, aligns the gears, and flicks a switch. Another robot blinks and sits up for the very first time. The robot stands and approaches the assembly line. Another robot clocks out and begins the long journey home.

A BRIEF HISTORY OF THE ICE AGE

The primates spot-checked their harpsichords, spoon-fed the plesiosaur, and garrisoned the tax collectors. They were ravenous, living inside a sarcophagus where steam engines glaciated into place, where imperial moths televised the impasse: the rickety mammoth confronting the equatorial scarecrow. The sabre-toothed polarity of the breeze exempted each neanderthal. The price war syncopated, the stellular vistas fallowed. Symphonies climaxed, entire marching bands faced extinction. Then, the great scraping—a gargantuan ice cube erasing the pyramids and the harpoonists, the lily pads, the approaching storm.

THE LOST CABIN

He sledded to the edge of the sky
like a careless child on rotten ice.
No food, no trail, no pinch of tobacco.
From among the gloomy spruce
a door slammed, and night fell. A strange sound
echoed through the dark. An eloquent howl,
pregnant with prophesy. How quickly he cooled!
Nevertheless, his cunning was wolf cunning,
wide-eyed and wide-eared to all that moved
about him. He was mastered by the verb *to eat*.
The thought struck him day after day, for days
unending, that the Lost Cabin seemed very near.
At nine o'clock he stubbed his toe. Soon
he would come to the land of tiny sticks.

A SIGN OF THE TIMES

My neighbour hammers a sign into his front yard:
PRIVATE PROPERTY NO TRESPASSING. His lawn is
just a tiny patch of grass—there's barely even room for
the sign. But he loves that patch of grass. He's out there
every night watering or mowing or just standing with
his eyes closed, breathing slowly and deeply like It's the
only place on earth where such peace is possible. All the
while I stare out the window, trying to tip him over with
my mind.

ELEVATOR

The doors open to sunrise over distant oceans. The doors open to a room of synchronized cuckoo clocks. The doors open to a riddle you could never solve. The doors open to a department store of glass eyes, all staring at you. The doors open to a corridor of mirrors, reflecting you to infinity. The doors open to explosions and screams for mercy. The doors open to the basement of your childhood, a flickering light bulb. The doors open to the ground rushing up to meet you. The doors open to a herd of wild horses galloping through a ghost town at midnight. The doors open to a black cat alone on the moon. The doors open to the contents of your refrigerator. The doors open to *Doctor Weep and Other Strange Teeth.* The doors open and suddenly it's raining and you forgot your umbrella. The doors open and you're gasping. The doors open to a total eclipse of the heart. The doors open to the Santa Claus Parade, the upside-down clowns of your nightmares. The doors open to a scarecrow wearing a business suit, typing on a computer with thin fingers of straw. The doors open to a room on fire. The doors open to the vast incoherencies of discourse. The doors open again. The doors open to swinging saloon doors, you drawing your revolver, squeezing the trigger, and fanning the hammer—smoke filling the room as whisky bottles explode and bandits leap for cover, overturning tables, scattering cards and poker chips. The doors open and the doctor says, "It's a boy!" The doors open to the inside of your mouth, a cavity in a molar. The doors open to numbness. The doors open to someone rushing down a long corridor yelling, "Hold that elevator!" but you don't. The doors open to a punch in the gut. The doors open to the frozen escapade of dawn. The doors open to a guttural chant, a room of records skipping. The doors open and you're nearly there. The doors open to elephants making love in a poem. The doors open to a herd of shopping carts on the great savannah. The doors open to terrible regret. The doors open to a mountain range in a blizzard, a robot trudging through knee-deep snow, lifting a torch to the night.

FROM EVERY CORNER

From every corner of the table, its own destiny:
strand of hair, single toothpick, a blue shadow,
and our host bravely eyeing the cur. Who cares,
we were thirsty—never setting foot in the tears.
All in one breath, a mild-mannered laugh lasts nightly.
There's an air among the petunias, silence declining
into the grapevine. A piano trills in that young air,
in the flickering night that dreams forget. Our patience
rambles on. Next, the billowing curtains, the lighting
of a cigarette, the atmosphere charmed. Going out
into the early hours, a delicate fingertip points
at the places of our youth, all those places with names.
Now, we cling to the nearest star and feign applause.

MOUSE

Every morning another sign: the pantry looted,
an avocado half-gnawed on the counter. You never
cleaned up after yourself. At night I could hear
the wall's innards being scaled, your scratching feet.

This morning you were trapped. A bag of dog food
nearly empty. The sides of the bag towered over you
as I peered in. You were hunched in a corner, nibbling
a piece of kibble, beady eyes, smoky fur.

I strapped you into the back seat of the car, tied
a small handkerchief over your eyes so you couldn't
find your way back. I drove into the country.
The late November leaves trailed behind.

Now when I write, my pen scratching the page
reminds me of you. I think back to that moment.
I was in the woods. You were in the palm of my hand,
perched on the edge of departure.

I never said goodbye.
And now that the nights have grown colder,
the days shorter, could you still survive the wilderness?
You are so small and the world has grown larger.

THE PERKS OF MISFORTUNE

I'm window-washing the skyscraper
because the rain won't clean it for us.
I squeegee each window and rappel
down its four sides. By the time I'm
finished, it's time to start again; some
bird has gone and made a mess of things.
From up here I see it all unfolding, the
dromedaries clambering over the hills,
the procession of bagpipers piping a dirge
for a fallen comrade. Just yesterday a faun
dove into the harbour for pearls but found only
day-old hotdogs discarded by their vendor.
There are real dogs peeing on hydrants and
taxidermists hailing taxicabs driven by deer.
A man with a briefcase sleeps in a phone booth.
A woman in heels beckons a pigeon to her
shoulder. A wild boar gores a police cruiser.
A sailboat stalls in an intersection without
even a breeze to speak of. The traffic builds.
The honking of horns rises, the honking of geese
descends, and I'm caught in the middle,
like some Greek god no one has ever heard of.

EVENING SIGHS

A house alone in the mountain-desert. A hand, half-hidden by the deepening shadow, stands at the entrance. A hand grinning.

A dog roves the wall. An instant of wolf. A window whistles wildly. In other rooms, the flimsy silence lingers.

The hand grips the doorknob. Teeth clatter to the floor. A possibility of fangs, the wolfish idea. The pile of blankets shivers.

FARMERS' MARKET

"How much for these rutabagas?" I asked the farmer. "Those rutabagas are fifty cents each," he said. "How about the carrots?" "They're three dollars a bunch." "And the turnips?" "Five hundred dollars each." "Why so much?" "Well sir, these turnips were grown in the fine pastures of Heaven and harvested by divine angels of light." I picked up one of the rooty vegetables and brushed off the dirt. It looked just like a regular turnip but I did feel holier, like my insides were glowing. I knew it was extravagant, but I was seriously considering the purchase. "Maybe I'll take one," I said, "I'll display it on my mantle for everyone to see." "You can't do that," the farmer said, "it'll just wither and mould. You've got to make a stew." "A five-hundred-dollar stew?" I asked, incredulous. "Sir," the farmer said, "that's a stew that will warm you from the inside out, a stew that will save your eternal soul."

THE ORACLE AND THE SCAPEGOAT

The Oracle weighed her options:
a marble gargoyle or a plaided frock.
Her Siamese twin found the choice tedious
and opted for the great heights of the fabled
saloon—she'd heard of a samurai who could
slice them down the middle. Their entire
lives they'd stared into the other's eyes and
felt the same heart twanging. It was time
to part, to hop away on a single leg and not
look back. The Scapegoat counted and recounted
her change. She'd scrounged enough for a bionic
heart, saved an old balloon to use as a second lung.
She gazed out the window at the herd of wildebeest
stampeding the ridge while the Oracle zigzagged her eyes
toward another window, through which she glimpsed
the future: an elegant pterodactyl soaring above the trees,
an overture for the descending frame of moonlight.

JUNKSHOP OF THE WORLD

Even to a high-flying bird, this was a country to be passed over quickly. Burned and browned, littered with fragments of rock and bone, the refuse of the making of the world. A passing shower drenched the bald range, and the slant morning sun set wet rocks aflame. The hills evaporated as the sun focused its gaze upon the desert. Cattle moved in a small bunch. Summer hunched their backs and arched their bellies. Overhead, an ominous black speck against the white-hot sky.

Over the hill came whistling fit for such a scene; it charmed those nameless rocks, changed them into a rough-coated wolf scanning the direction from which the whistle drew. A horseman rode out of that glance. A thin, handsome face—eyes and black hair—a body tall but slender. A red bandana knotted around his throat. The rider seemed in tune with mighty distances, that cruel sun, and the bird of prey hovering high, high in the air.

The horse he bestrode was a statue in black marble. To see the horse was to forget all else. His flanks shimmered. Only a poet could run fifteen hands over the matchless curves, the legs of carefully drawn steel, that flow of tail and windy mane, generous breast, mighty heart, arched neck, proud head, pricking ears, wide forehead and muzzle. The rider urged the horse slowly toward the wolf and dismounted.

A rustle like dried leaves came from among the rocks and the wolf's hackles rose. Sniffing, he turned. A long rattler slid out from beneath a boulder, ready to strike. The man growled. He drew a short knife no human had ever used. His feet poised. The rattler tucked and struck. The cowboy flashed.

Then, he performed the most ordinary act— he stepped into his horse. Contrary to the rules, the stallion did not flinch, but surrounded the rider entirely. The man let go his own ears, his nose, his shoulder. The wolf stared into the horse and nodded. The horse galloped down the easy slope and quickly faded into dust.

The episode was silent as a moment lost among hills. But the whistling returned, fainter and fainter, until it was only a whisper that dwelt in the air.

MY MOTHER THE FLY

Every day my mother appeared smaller,
more fragile. Hunched over her walker,
she'd hobble around the kitchen as if on six legs.
Her hair draped over her shoulders, so white
it was nearly transparent, so light even a slight
breeze would lift it and cause it to glimmer.
As her vision diminished, her glasses thickened,
magnifying her eyes, taking up half her face.
Sometimes, I'd shout just so she could hear me—
the buzzing of her hearing aids filled the room.

One night a loud roar startled me awake.
I crawled out of bed and stumbled downstairs.
There she was, in her nightgown and slippers,
vacuuming the windowsill. "Mother," I called out,
"it's three in the morning. What are you doing?"
She turned to me with tears in her eyes.
"There's flies," she said, "they're all dead."
I took her by the arm and led her back to bed.
I'd just turned out the lights when I noticed
the old photo album lying on her bedside table,
and resting on the open page, her dentures
still glowing, somehow smiling.

THE ROBOT AND THE STONE

After a long day at the factory, the robot arrives home and discovers a stone abandoned on the front steps. The robot lifts the stone gently, careful to not disturb its slumber. The robot gives the stone a bed to sleep in. It feeds and clothes the stone. The robot gives the stone a formal education; it raises the stone as if it were its own. The stone grows older, harder and more reserved. It never speaks or makes kind gestures. Still, the robot tucks the stone in every night. It kisses the stone and whispers, "Sweet dreams, sleep tight."

TRIMMING THE KING'S BEARD

I discover the peanut that never made it to his mouth, the arrow halted in its trajectory. I reveal the map of the hidden passageway, the key to the catacombs. I keep trimming and retrieve his chain mail hauberk, his ornate broadsword. I uncover a silver goblet and a flagon of mulberry wine. I untangle his Andalusian stallion and snip away a clearing for its pasture. I stumble upon the lost regiment of men-at-arms, stricken with scurvy. I sharpen my scissors and continue clipping away the wilderness. I unveil a rolling meadow dotted with windmills, a dark castle rising. I lather and shave the mountainous ridge of his jaw, pluck the last overgrown forest from his eyebrows. When the kingdom of his chin is smooth, he cradles a nest of meadowlarks, featherless and crying for food. "Can I keep them?" he implores.

TAPESTRY OF AN ORDINARY DAY

Eagerly this morning I walloped umpires.
Their armour rasped, their tape recorders whined.
Their sludge was ravenous. I rocket-launched
out of beggardry and pummelled into oncoming wisdom.
Shimmering knights rigged daggers. The rain tapped at
its wineglass. For a while, I tracked my dogged mother,
then I traded my dog for a wallflower. The slab was blue,
the sky was blunt. I rolled out of bedlam
and put on my slippers without Socrates,
something I rarely document. I magnetised coffee
and siphoned it while skating on the couch. I putted
a sigh. It ricocheted off a dour walrus and plummeted
into the wise men's static, the night's ragged domicile.

PORTRAIT OF A STRANGER ON A TRAIN IN A DREAM

Your eyes are twin oceans the size of grapes. Your nose is a mountain on the verge of collapse. Your smile, a twisted branch of a gnarled tree. Your laugh, the jingle of loose change in my pocket. Your eyebrows contort to question marks. Your ears are freshly baked cinnamon buns. Your right scapula, the continent of Africa. Your calves are baby cows. Your thighs are a phone ringing without answer. Your hair is spaghetti. Your breasts are corrosive and properly labelled to inform and deter. Your kidneys are kidney beans. Your feet, a bed of red coals. Your spinal column is Romanesque. Your left scapula, sculpted by Michelangelo. Your lips, a palate of oil-based paint. Your teeth, a string of blinking Christmas lights. Your voice is the sound of distant traffic. Your neck, a deep well of sorrow. Your hands are the windows of a train. Your arms are the landscape flashing past. Your heart is that hill in the distance. Your shadow is the oak tree without leaves standing alone in a sudden summer downpour.

TOTALLY COMPULSIVE BEHAVIOUR

I'd bitten my fingernails
right down to the skin,
so I chewed off each finger
and gnawed away the palm of my hand.
Then I devoured both forearms.
I couldn't reach my elbows,
so I flexed my body backwards
and pointed my toes.
I'll admit it was snake-like,
the way my jaw unhinged,
the way my feet entered my gullet
and I worked my way upward,
swallowing my knees, then my torso.
When I felt my teeth gripping
the back of my skull,
I knew I'd gone too far.
I peeked out from behind my teeth
as I closed my mouth
like a single, giant eyelid.

LITTORAL INTERLUDE

1.

There, in the foreground,
a spastic hermit crab
I mistook
for a shard of light.

2.

Up in the sky,
the ground.
Down here,
the ground.

3.

It was true:
whatever I'd lost.

4.

The sand seeped
through the cracks
between my fingers—
the beach
was running out.

5.

Footsteps
fell
like
raindrops.

6.

I threw up.

7.

White moon overhead,
a toenail clipping
on the rim of the tub.

||

It was a black dog with yellow-gold spots where its eyebrows should have been.

— John Steinbeck

FISTICUFFS

He strikes my nose with an ivory gavel.
I singe his moustache with a flaming baton.
He tramples my toes with a procession of pachyderms.
I sting his cheeks with a thousand aggravated hornets.
He clobbers my kidneys like they're punching bags.
I lunge with a ballpoint pen. He defends with a down pillow
and smites me with a tornado of hammers. My head bobbles.
His clenched fists rocket from his forearms, uppercut my chin,
knock me out of my boots. I recline slowly into the air,
time inflating beneath me like a bag of microwave popcorn.
Then his crumpling blow; a waterfall of bowling balls
cascades into my gut, splays me to the ground.
He aims a kicking horse at my already splintered ribcage,
but like a dice I roll away, dropping a perfectly timed
banana peel beneath his foot. His arms flail like frantic
windmills—he totters. I heft my grandfather's bazooka
and launch a giant wad of chewing gum, which engulfs
him from the waist down. He struggles, but remains.
I summon a javelin of lightning and hurl it, skewering
his heart like a shish kebab. His eyes flash,
then dim. For a moment there is only the wind
bending the grass. He topples. Trumpets sprout
from the blood-speckled earth and regale my throbbing ears.
I smile though my teeth are dominoes, dominoes.

THE ROBOT'S FAVOURITE PASTIME

A robot sits beside the fireplace and stares into the flames. Hours pass and the robot doesn't blink. The logs crackle, sparks ascend. The flames are hypnotic. They waver with visions of what's to come: a fork in the road, a wolf sleeping beneath an oak, three crows squawking directions. Falling snow will fill the robot's footprints. There will be no turning back. The robot will cross a desert, a mountain, and a four-lane highway. It will be charred by the relentless sun, blasted by icy gales, and honked at by tractor trailers. The robot will come to a meadow. The body of a robot will be rusting at its feet. A payphone will ring. A cannon will fire. The robot will answer.

THE PRESSURES OF PUBLIC OFFICE

The train has yet to arrive. On the platform and waiting, a single slice of apple pie. No fancy plate, no fine cutlery. The pie does not move or speak. Commuters bustle past, and though their mouths water, they don't dare take a bite. Instead, they tip their hats and say, "Good morning, Mr. Mayor."

The election had been a landslide. The pie did not make empty promises. It exuded confidence, not straying from the issues at hand. During debates, its silence was resolute. Signs read A CANDIDATE JUST LIKE GRANDMA USED TO BAKE. The pie appeared at every press conference and political rally. Its crust was particularly photogenic.

And now, as the train departs, the pie sits in a window seat. It does not look up as the conductor requests its ticket, nor does it look out the window. The slice of pie does not see the woman standing on the platform, teary-eyed, waving a handkerchief. She knows the mayor will not be coming back, that a crumb and the scent of cinnamon are all she has left.

THE POSSUM'S SNEEZE

Horses sing because it is night.
I once knew their music, their croon.
Tigers drift in the balmy night,
the sound of cutlery rubbing,
a sink full of cigarettes. The moon's
potbelly navigates a tight shirt.
Worms translate the night by crawling
into heels and stepping into eternity.
I erase history, paint snow.
Stones turn, looking for the night,
asking for it with their voices.
The stones discover rain in galleries
and possums fossilizing in my chest.
It is night. The horses are singing.
The sky flickers with a faulty connection.
I've been trying to write you for days.

THE WOODSMAN

On the bank of the stream, I meet a hunter. His gun is moss-covered, his beard thick with foliage. He says he has been lost for years. I tell him he is not far from the village and I can show him the way back. He smiles a toothless grin and says he's been away too long to go back. He now understands the nature of change, leaves turning from green to red as he blinks. I grab his arm to lead him, but the limb snaps off in my hand. The hunter looks at me with knotted eyes and shakes his head. The air grows cold. The wood needs splitting. I lift my axe and swing. He smiles a toothless grin and tells me he has been lost for years.

THE GREAT EXPLORATION

The farmer picks his nose and discovers a small planet spinning on the tip of his finger. He squints to see what's going on. A Viking longship sails beyond the headlands, an old collie barks into the far distance. A golden eagle plunges from the sky and snags the dog in its talons. The wind whips into a frenzy, tears corn from the fields. The river runs dry and the earth cracks with thirst. Another catastrophe picks up where the previous one leaves off: barbarian invasion, plague of locusts, forty days of rain. The farmer doesn't know how it all started, or when it will end, or why there's nothing he can do but sit and watch.

THE SAVAGE IS A MAESTRO

Beyond the falling mountains,
clouds composed of sneakers.
Laces dangle like vines on which
baboons swing every hour, on the hour.

It's well past midnight
when the folded cranes
sail in through the window,
fluttering hand-written wings.

An enormous wave exhibits its torpor,
ventures inward, a blue collision.
A smudge of lemon meringue,
its opulent, seraphim glow.

THE VANISHED BUTTONS TRILOGY

1. THE LONG JOURNEY

Big Red trudged the arduous slope. Ahead was the mountain, and all around nothing but prairie and sky. While the country stretched, Big Red plodded on, trying to recall everything. Once, he glimpsed antelope, but they disappeared among waves. He saw the grey buffalo, Mr. Flight-of-Bones. He saw something growing among the dark. Mr. Afire was asleep on the grass, half-eaten bird in his hand. Big Red approached. Mr. Afire stirred. The two made a grand fire. At night they sat by the fire and told stories of the mountain and the wagon. The wind passed through the dead pines. Big Red heard it like a whisper. "Don't be afraid," it said, "it's only the wind."

2. THE MOUNTAIN

The trouble with the mountain was in all directions, but it was the best Big Red had seen in days. He put himself in the mind of the mountain, thought of each hour by itself. He figured the mountain saw deer and buffalo, herds of elk and wild horses, but there were no skulls afoot. He thought of the tress along the ridge, the dead pines. He thought of the mountain listening to the wind and looking out into the darkening sky. The endless plain. A small fire poking a hole into the night...

3. THE WAGON

Big Red lost all track of time and Mr. Afire was fading. Then came a sound. It might have been the river or the cool wind gusting out of the north, the voice of a coyote, a tin can tossed among rocks, the rasping pines, the crackling fire, or the creaking of wooden tires. It was the creaking of wooden tires. It was the wagon. It was the wagon carrying the river or the cool wind gusting out of the north. The wagon crying like a coyote. The wagon illumed in silver moonlight. It approached the fire and Big Red gathered his belongings. He climbed inside and curled on the grey buffalo hide. But where was Mr. Afire? Hiding beneath a boulder? Big Red closed his eyes and deliberately whispered a deep, sound sleep. And as the wagon bumped along into the night, the rain began. It fell upon the powdery dust, over the dead pines and the rocks. It fell where he had walked and slowly his tracks disappeared, bit by bit, under the caressing touch of the rain.

WHERE EMPTY SLEEVES ECHO

The pork chop lies naked in the snake's gullet.
The kangaroo licks its blood-red lips.

On Thursday, the Argonauts eat fish sticks.
The fields overrun with sloth.

A submarine breaches in a Jacuzzi.
A clown drowns in the ocean.

The moon breaks from its cocoon.
A mountain goat swoons on the tip of a tooth.

Friday night rains umbrellas.
Sunday wakes with tumbleweeds rolling right through it.

Every star is a micro-speck of star.
A coffin is filled with jelly donuts.

A vacuum inhales its own power cord.
A snowman picks its nose with a carrot.

Inside the juice box, I touch the ceiling.
A headless mannequin holds the lantern.

A shaman plods along Boulevard de Sébastopol.
A pair of pants pants in this heat.

The attic bursts into fireflies.
Yonder murmurs in amazement.

THE BLACK PLANET

The Black Planet gleamed ahead of me. It was a strange place—jungles of concrete gaping upward and people with teeth like tombstones. Their smiles were the disastrous kind, the kind that open old wounds and the rush hour traffic piles in. I still pointed west, watching mountains grow from mere bumps on the ground. I placed my plasma rifle between my knees and checked it over—only fourteen pulses left. That wouldn't get me far. Strapping on my rucksack, I tiptoed across the derelict shadows, drove halfway across the planet. I broke a promise to myself, but forgave myself instantly. There was no need to fuss, no need to cause unwarranted panic among my ten billion body cells. What if they suddenly refused to co-operate? What if they decided to go their own separate ways, splitting me apart in ten billion directions at once? Where exactly would I be at the end of the day?

THE ROBOT'S PART-TIME JOB

The robot's job is to count the sheep on a hill. The robot counts one sheep on the hill. The sheep eats grass and hardly moves. The robot counts it again. One white sheep, one green hill. A bluebird alights on a nearby branch and the robot listens to it warble. Again. One sheep still eating. The robot sits on a rock beneath the oak. A colony of ants scurries in the shade. The robot counts three thousand seven hundred and sixty-seven ants. The robot looks up. Night has fallen and the sheep is gone.

THE FINE PRINT

The most dissonant violin
is a clavicle of moonlight.
You are walking through a passage
in a novel no one ever wrote. Here,
a blade of ice chides the human mind,
a contraption tears at the sky.

Wisped as fine print, the ghost of
a horse grazing in the backyard
of every house you've ever known.
Do you weep every morning, or is
the cement truck filled with envelopes?
A great wind lifts the squealing wheels.

Thus, a mirror ripens with sunlight.
Letters are delivered, but only
as simple afterthoughts, like
tiny fishing boats or freighters
in the distance. If I said you were
a monsoon, would that make it so?

The floor sags but won't discuss
the cannibalistic ways of absence,
the wind thrashing the magnolia.
The mountain is telling its life story.
Blossoms frantic in the hourglass.

THE SHAPE OF THINGS TO COME

A black cloud swirls over our city, a swarm of flies so thick it blocks out the sun. We're plunged into one unending night, but no one sleeps for the ever-present drone. The moment dinner is served, the flies descend and ravage the meal. We're left making thin soups with whatever bones we can find. Our repellents are futile. Our coils of flypaper remain bare. We swat at the flies, but they zip past like tiny spaceships at red alert. They're evolving faster than we are. Soon we'll be the ones buzzing around the streets looking for something to believe in.

AN INVENTORY OF THE SOUL

A one-ton chandelier. A head plus a hat on a stage. Shelves overstocked with two-for-the-price-of-one puddles, mouths brimming with rain.

The head speaks of this perpetual autumn. The jester versus the lion. A trunk of antler bone. A chasm's shadow box and stacks of unpaid phone bills.

A masquerade at the lumber mill. My silhouette on fire. A bowl of black jujubes. A hat for the head. The head in my hands.

THE ROCKING HORSE AND THE FLOOD

The wooden horse swayed in the breeze. The rain continued. The smell of wet cement was replaced with the fragrance of ocean. There was no plug to be pulled and the tide rose quickly. The sidewalk sprouted seaweed, cars gargled and sputtered. The wooden horse reared on, galloping over the waves, its mane glistening, teeth painted into a smile. Our neighbour was building a raft out of garbage cans, but it was too late; the horse had rocked out of sight, its wooden hooves splashing like a child in a puddle.

WRITING BY STREETLIGHT

An old shopping cart tipped over in the weeds.
It's missing a wheel and starting to rust. It already
creaks in the wind. Yellow leaves scatter
like crumpled-up parking tickets. A plastic bag
ignores the walk signal's flashing hand. For a while,
there's just the wind, the lampposts and their ideas,
a red mountain bike rattling its chain, a fire hydrant
sitting like an obedient golden retriever, a payphone
longing for someone to talk to. In the park two benches
face one another and can't turn away. The garbage cans
remain insatiable. The wind waves the flags
and the flags wave the black flags of their shadows.
The darkening windows reflect on everything
they've seen, the reruns of past seasons and how
it's all come to this. Beneath the streetlight
the newly fallen rain sparkles like broken glass.

GROCERY DAY

The two boys from next door are outside, playing cops and robbers. As I finish unloading the car, they run up to me. "Where'd you get those?" the officer asks, pointing to the bags. "Must've robbed a bank," the other boy explains. "They're just groceries, honest," I say. The officer makes a gun of his thumb and index finger, aims it at my chest, and says, "Put up your hands." But the bags are too heavy, I can't lift them above my head. He smiles and says, "Bang! Bang!" I double over, say, "Ooh, you got me," and they laugh. I stumble and fall. I writhe on my back and roll to my stomach. They are in hysterics. I force a cough and feel faint. On hands and knees, I reach for my stomach, see red on the tips of my fingers. My teeth chatter. The boys howl. I lie on my back, head lolling sideways. Slowly a jar of pickles rolls toward the curb, where it teeters precariously.

GOODBYE

Your retirement home on the moon, your Stradivarius clouds.
Your garden of sea glass, your ocean of sand.
Your goldfish that outgrew its bowl and sated its hunger.
Your jade fruit fly, your lawnmower made of grass.
Your long-standing ties to the community, your antique kitten.
Your forgotten birthday come back to haunt you.
Your sinking boat, your town crier's voice box.
Your catastrophic meltdown, your baby left on a doorstep.
Your dry cough in a desert.
Your hunched-back best friend with a broken wristwatch.
Your cobblestone sky, your moth-eaten umbrella.
Your card-shuffling gait, your suburb of cedar.
Your parrot speaking in a foreign tongue.
Your septic system of deep sleep.
Your grandmother's teacup that opens its mouth as wide
    as a four-lane highway.
Your Greyhound bus that appears
    as you write a farewell letter, dipping your pen
into the inkwells of my eyes.
    You fold the universe and slip it into an envelope.
You loved me.

A PARABLE

If your friend is a sheep, do not eat him when evening falls. If he is a spider, he will teach you the art of gathering dust. If he is a window facing the sea. If you require safe passage, trust the one-eyed ferryman. On the crest of every hill, the wolf. Inside each wolf, a flock of sheep. Every sheep is a cloud in the blue meadow of sky. Give the ferryman a quarter and he will use it to start the machine. If you are a machine. If you are machine, he will start you with a quarter. If the sheep require safe passage. On the crest of each wave, the wolf. Inside each wolf, the wolf. If your friend is a wolf, do not eat the sky. If he is the art of gathering dust, he may be a cloud. If he is a spider with one eye. If he is when evening falls. If he is a window facing the sea.

POEM FOR A DOG

There was that time we were camping
in a thunderstorm. Every few seconds
the sky lit up our tent, but you slept
right through, rolling to your side.
Your heavy sigh making the world
a better place, while reminding my heart
of its constant state of disrepair.
Tomorrow is another day with you,
but it's also one day less. There are still
so many undiscovered streets,
stars whose light has not yet reached us.
We're barely begun to breathe.
Every fire burns to the same conclusion:
the small mound that remains. Aren't we the same?
The sound of rain on the roof of the tent.
The thunder rippling the lake. Earlier,
I wrote poems on its shoreline.
You dug a hole and rolled in sand.
The sky clouded and we started the long hike
back to the campsite. You were far ahead,
nose to the ground, occasionally glancing
over your shoulder to make sure I was still there.

THE ROBOT RIDES A BUS

While crossing the street, a robot is hit by a bus. Small parts of the robot roll down a hill, frayed wires spark, lights flash. The bus driver kneels beside the robot and cries, "If I were a mechanic, you'd be repaired. If I were a priest, you'd be blessed." The robot attempts to raise an arm, but there is only the grinding of gears, the leaking of oil. The robot tries to speak, but its voice is garbled and growing faint. Silence envelops the scene. A robot lies in the street. A crowd gathers. The driver, still on his knees, cradles the robot's dented head. The crowd closes in and hoists the robot to its shoulders. In a short procession, they enter the bus. The driver wipes his eyes with a heavy sleeve and follows. The doors close. The bus lurches into gear and continues down the rolling hills, towards a lake that is always in the distance.

WILD TURKEYS

In the middle of the night, I woke and stared out the window as if I were a long-lost friend. The next morning I sat over an empty bowl, head lowered. I pushed open the screen door and called to my parents across the lawn. I pointed to the last white house at the end of the row of white houses. "What about him?" I asked. "He's missing," replied my mother. I cried until dinnertime. "Yesterday, come home," I said, watching the trees shake.

UNIVERSE COMPOSED OF MOSTLY NOTHING, NEW STUDY INDICATES

Suddenly we're weightless,
columns of light
slice through us
and a gentle breeze
blows us further apart.
For a while we drift,
waving farewell to our hands,
whispering goodbye
with lips already distant
to ears that were barely even here.

NOTES

"The Same Old Story" borrows its first line from Catie Rosemurgy's poem "Miss Peach: A Historical Reenactment" which appeared in *The Stranger Manual*. "Act of God" was inspired by *The Old Timers of Gun Shy* by Jim Miller. "The Lost Cabin" borrows lines and phrases from *Jack London Unabridged*. "From Every Corner" was written while listening to John Ashbery read in Chicago on November 17, 1973. "Evening Sighs" borrows from *The Untamed* by Max Brand. "Junkshop of the World" is a modified erasure poem from the first chapter of the same book. "The Possum's Sneeze" is a response to the poem "I ache sometimes, from loving this world so much, from loving" by Jessica Hiemstra. "The Vanished Buttons Trilogy" began as an erasure poem from *Down the Long Hills* by Louis L'Amour. "The Black Planet" was inspired by *The Secret of the Black Planet* by Milton Lesser. "The Fine Print" was written while listening to John Ashbery read "The Skaters" at the Washington Square Art Gallery, NYC, August 23, 1964. "An Inventory of the Soul" is a mistranslation of "Le Vent Et L'esprit" by Pierre Reverdy. "Goodbye" was written after "Hello" by Benjamin Peret (translated by Michael Benedikt). "Wild Turkeys" is a modified erasure poem from chapter 19 of Goosebumps #14 *The Werewolf of Fever Swamp* by R.L. Stine.

ACKNOWLEDGEMENTS

Earlier versions of some of these poems have appeared in *Arc, The Rusty Toque, Sterling, The Puritan, Lemon Hound, Tracer, BafterC, Translating Horses, and The KFPL Poetry Blackboard*. Thank you to the appropriate editors.

Many of these poems benefited from the writer-in-residence programs at Queen's University and Kingston Frontenac Public Library. Thank you to Carolyn Smart, Stuart Ross, Steven Heighton, and Helen Humphreys.

I am grateful to the Ontario Arts Council for their support through the Writers' Reserve Program.

Thank you to: Everyone at Invisible Publishing who helped make this book possible, especially Leigh Nash for the time and care you've taken with my manuscript, your gentle and precise edits, and for your insight into my writing; this book wouldn't exist without you. Writers and friends for encouragement, conversation, and camaraderie over the years, especially Stuart Ross, Cameron Anstee, Christine Miscione, Jason Heroux, Nelson Ball, Brandon Crilly, Bruce Kauffman, and Gary Barwin. Nicholas Papaxanthos for collaboration in poetry and friendship. Andrew Nurse for inspiring me to publish my first chapbook. Bryan Greer and Brandon Root for attending every single reading I gave in Peterborough. My family for all your love and support. Allison for your endless inspiration, patience, and love: this book is for you.

INVISIBLE PUBLISHING is a not-for-profit publishing company that produces contemporary works of fiction, creative non-fiction, and poetry. We're small in scale, but we take our work, and our mission, seriously: We publish material that's engaging, literary, current, and uniquely Canadian.

We are committed to publishing diverse voices and experiences. In acknowledging historical and systemic barriers, and the limits of our existing catalogue, we strongly encourage writers of colour to submit their work.

Invisible Publishing continues to produce high-quality literary works, and we're also home to the Bibliophonic series, Snare, and Throwback imprints.

If you'd like to know more please get in touch:
info@invisiblepublishing.com

Invisible Publishing
Halifax & Picton